This is What the Desert Surrenders

Also by Shaun T. Griffin

Woodsmoke, Wind, and the Peregrine
Winter in Pediatrics
Bathing in the River of Ashes
Snowmelt

Limited Editions

Under Red-Tailed Sky
Words I Lost at Birth

Editions

The River Underground: An Anthology of Nevada Fiction
Torn by Light: Selected Poems of Joanne de Longchamps
Desert Wood: An Anthology of Nevada Poets

Translation

Death to Silence. Poems by Emma Sepúlveda

This Is What the Desert Surrenders

NEW AND SELECTED POEMS

Shaun T. Griffin

Rainshadow Editions
The Black Rock Press
University of Nevada, Reno
2012

ISBN: 978-1-891033-61-2

Library of Congress Control Number: 2012946023

Printed in the United States of America

The Black Rock Press
University of Nevada, Reno
Reno, NV 89557-0224
www.blackrockpress.org

Cover art by Jeff Nicholson
Detail from "Hard to Stay Grounded"
Oil on canvas

for Richard, Carolyn, and Hayden

and my family—
Debby, Nevada, and Cody

Contents

from Snowmelt

from BATHING IN THE RIVER OF ASHES

from Winter in Pediatrics

from Woodsmoke, Wind, and the Peregrine

Acknowledgments

The author is grateful to the following publishers for permission to reprint the following poems, some of which appeared in a slightly different form: "Letter to My Wife from the Coastal Plain, Arctic National Wildlife Refuge" in *The Texas Observer;* "Reading Jeffers in the Rainy January Dawn" in *Jeffers Studies;* "Letter from the Hood River Shallows" in *Isotope;* "Running to Southern California" in *Red Thread Gold Thread* (anthology); "Los Vendedores" in *Writers Forum;* "Rain Outside Lovelock, Late March" in *The Comstock Review;* "The Fallen Season" in *The Clifden Anthology* (Ireland); "The Meth Addict Out My Window" and "Heron Dance" in *Poets of the American West* (anthology); and "Daffodils One Sunday Before Snow," in *The Fourth River*; to Robert L. Reid for his quote from *Mountains of the Great Blue Dream* which appeared in "The Last Songbird on Malta"; to e. e. cummings for his quote from "in Just-" in *100 Selected Poems* which appeared in the "Grey Elliot Riff"; and to Hayden Carruth for his quote from "40" in *The Sleeping Beauty* which appeared in "Waking from the Charcoal Dark."

Special thanks also to the following presses for permission to reprint poems from the following books:

Snowmelt, Black Rock Press, 1994.
Bathing in the River of Ashes, University of Nevada Press, 1999.
"Winter in Pediatrics," included in *The Harvest of Lesser Burdens: Art in the Fields of Medicine,* Nevada Museum of Art Press, 2006.
Woodsmoke, Wind, and the Peregrine, Black Rock Press, Reno, Nevada, 2008.

Finally, my heartfelt thanks to Tom Meschery, whose careful reading winnowed these poems from their many roots.

Foreword

The most instructive and succinct introduction I could write would be simply to say: Lovers of lyric poetry, whatever you do, get this collection of poems by Shaun Griffin and read it. The poems will thoroughly delight you.

Succinct and instructive, but in no way illuminating. The subtlety and beauty contained within these pages deserve a great deal more.

The poet Paul Engle said, "Poetry is boned with ideas, nerved and blooded with emotion, and held together by the delicate and tough skin of words." The more I read the poems in this collection, the more I harkened back to Engle's words. In Shaun's poems the elements of idea, emotion, and language come together to form a unity of immense power. I am certain Engle would be impressed by them.

How so? First and foremost, Shaun Griffin compresses such a multitude of emotions into so few lines, a feat of poetic packaging I have rarely witnessed. This does not mean that Shaun is a minimalist, even though in many of his poems he does flirt with this approach to poetry. In some instances, I found myself thinking of Denise Levertov. Like Levertov, Shaun achieves intellectual and emotional density through specificity of language. You cannot read the poems in this collection without paying careful attention not only to each word, but to each syllable and how they are grafted together to create-like a plant biologist's hybrid-an altogether new and powerful lyric. Shaun Griffin's devotion to the lyrical voice makes this book stunningly pleasing.

Not that Shaun eschews the narrative. The first poem in this collection, for example, "My Sons Who Have No Opera to Console Them," begins with the following lines: "Pavarotti lies in a hospital bed,/and my sons who have no opera/to console them, pulled from the driveway./I held them in the garage without words." A few pages further on in the collection we find the poem "Reading Jeffers in the Rainy January Dawn." The lines in this poem nod in the direction of a narrative: "worse for us, he wrote/through the durance of two wars,/with melancholy to guide from shorebird to stone.../then died." Many of the poems in the section *Winter in Pediatrics* (2006) also tend heavily toward the narrative. But while Shaun Griffin gives us idea and character, he never strays too far from the highly emotional (lyrical) voice that, in my mind, is his greatest strength.

It is this constant pulling back from the brink of the narrative (ideas of people, events, and history) and turning the poem over to the emotional and lyrical that constitutes the second most important quality of this collection. My own taste in poems has always run to the ones that tell stories. If some of the lines go a bit flat, I am willing to let the poem walk instead of soar. In Shaun's poetry I never find that I have to make a choice. He tells the story without ever given up the lyrical integrity of the poem. Rhythm is never sacrificed for meaning. Take this opening stanza from "Woman Empty": "On her heart/a growth flames/with hatred/In a room, numb with men/she is too weak/for the stench of passion." I am ready to enter a sad tale, but I know I will hear it to the accompaniment of some musical instrument-say, a muted trumpet.

Some of the finest and most Griffinesque poetry comes from his latest book: *Woodsmoke, Wind, and the Peregrine* (2008). Here, I find Shaun Griffin turning himself over to the pulse of nature, and like the birds that are the subjects of this book, allowing himself to soar.

It is not a coincidence that I began this introduction by quoting from two poems in the section devoted to Shaun's new poems. They are the voice of a mature poet and are therefore extremely pleasing to one who has witnessed the various stages of Shaun Griffin's poetic growth. In order to enjoy the new poems better, I suggest you save the first section until last. You will then be able to better appreciate the subtlety of this line from

"Letter from the Hood River Shallows," which is written for his wife, Debby, on her fiftieth birthday. I am stunned by it: "Close to the moon of many egrets," that last plural echoing through all the marriages of the world, successful or not. Be prepared for these kinds of surprises in the new poems.

In its entirety, be prepared to enjoy the ideas, the emotions, and the words in *This Is What the Desert Surrenders*.

—Tom Meschery

New Poems

My Sons Who Have No Opera to Console Them

Pavarotti lies in a hospital bed,
and my sons who have no opera

to console them, pulled from the driveway.

I held them in the garage without words—
poet who could say nothing—

and my hands, the empty tools of fatherhood—

chased their bikes from the greasy floor,
fished laundry from the pile,

and dressed the wild room for a guest.

There was nothing to recall
but pictures and stones we climbed

in the dusted wind. And if I gave them tools

to scale some mountain other than this one
where their twenty-odd years were spent,

they were shed like teeth on a saw blade.

We emptied our pockets this day
the opera cried, *Luciano,* but I wanted

the sound of boys in a garage of sawdust,

the wood chiseled to ants, leaves, and a last,
prescient glow in the mirror, when the youngest ate

the image of his father, shoulders away.

Letter from the Hood River Shallows

for Debby at fifty

Close to the moon of many egrets—
opal, orange, obsidian, she rose
by the river of wind and bird, refuge

to a man in the sanctuary of this gorge,
the mask of gulls and rotted wood
in the rocks that mark her half-century—

the age of bones licked to shore
in the serpentine currents and I imagine
ours will end in the mountain home—

stretched to every complication
like the locusts she detests, helpless scribes
with no water to breathe these birds

in the foment of raspberries
and willows that light the shallows
of some other land long withheld—

this night of her turning to fall,
the red-orange eclipse of leaves and dew
and us—so many waters from shore.

Reading Jeffers in the Rainy January Dawn

Reading Jeffers in the rainy January dawn,
what is to say that stone and bird and tree cannot—
        because like Whitman before him,
he was a guest of the cliff, the gull, the leaf,
and—worse for us, he wrote
        through the durance of two wars,
        with melancholy to guide from shorebird to stone—
then died, a deer laid down to coast water. And, without
sanctuary, memorized the trinity of flora, fauna,
and we, however inhuman—
        raked back to ourselves. Of course he lost faith:

        we strove to divide the words
from the man on the seacoast who stood like Machado,
the ancients, the mothers keening
        under the weight of anguish and light—
a man apart from the abacus of time and state
        that gilded now, could not destroy.
Impatient, humbled, sonorous poet, he chose
the stones, the birds, and the trees to venerate
        beauty and truth—the delirious constant
in the new world: no man without them.

Leaving Hunger in the American West

For two days we sat at the edge of hunger,
Carmelites at the insurrection—

a lake beyond the conference window

and the Canadian geese flew to the gray
water at meeting's end as if it were blood

below feathers and the stone washing began:

who among willows deserves crayfish
or pine nuts washed to the shallows

of questions we could not answer?

Tonight my son will come home to scour
the pantry and I will feed him, and the geese

their young, but the many for whom we met

walk without a lake, a willow stem to lie below—
and the journey to sea is begun: we are

the ministers of freedom and recollection,

a zephyr below a wing or a child
except, of course, I speak for no hunger

and then the vile refrain: you have come

too far with your knowledge. The heart
become serpent and so touch water

for sustenance: cold, clear, willing

to breach the back of my hands—almost
anonymous in the thresh of hands not held.

Rain Outside Lovelock, Late March

The first whiskers poke

from greasewood.

Clouds sulk the ridge beyond

an alfalfa farm.

A roadside cross pretends to grieve

and the few willows reach to

Rye Patch, a last body

of water before the dry, endless miles.

This could be the road to Inuvik

yet there is no warrior

at the horizon. The landscape is quarantined:

a desert peach offers pink rosaries

to the slopes bladed for minerals,

once white and hard with tranquility,

now dust in the atmosphere.

This is what the desert surrenders

to the magpie bloated on the centerline,

to fresh prints at the petroglyphs,

to the feral galaxy of spring.

The Meth Addict Out My Window

lives with his arthritic father,
third in his class at Cal—
a civil engineer, whose hand
I opened at the post office
a hundred times, and who, without a son,
stood near upright until he came home
to glitter the moon to its inky death,
the bulb burning in his eyes,
the translucent one, porch-stooped,
smoking gun, always lit
for the fun in his half-naked den—

and mother ravels the reeds of her kin,
tiny volume of misanthropes,
the son she avows
in her loft at night—
to kiss this bulb awry
would miscarry her mind to gin—and he

scoots the morning sun
to clean the Harley frame,
a motorcycle not quite
in the imaginary turn at 80—
girl pressed to his ribs like a throttle
to the great wide open of we

who've become his neighbors
that will not disturb him,
positioned on the crank
of every move, until he juts out
like a mole—for whom light
is darkness and food,
something to fear—

when my wife calls to confide
the dogs sniffing the yard,
the pale blue assault of uniforms
carting their prize away
from this, our town of sleep and decay:

what we need in the night
to frisk the anguish of love,
this hour removed
from his ordeal in the house like fire
for the two who no longer sleep
the worry downstairs, and so begin
to scissor his picture from the paper,
press the hornet eyes in a drawer,
and scavenge the nightstand
for a face to endure.

A Leaf at the Board of Pardons

For Bobby

I

I sit in the resplendent shadow of sun,
unjudged by the warmth, the blue light
that begins with dawn. All week

I managed the melancholy of meetings
and Tuesday, heard the breath of legal gods
pronounce merciful judgment on my friend

in prison for the duration. How does
sun come to him now—through the speckled
bars of triumph that only yesterday

built the shelter of no regret—and
if a man can return to such light,
such repose in the calm of this Friday

before Thanksgiving, is there any reason
to hope for the light beyond his cave?
There is—only the blue and white tendrils

will bend steel to release him, crush
the moonlit dark that for decades,
confined him to wander the lunar cliff.

II

I think of Su Tung-p'o in the court of moonlight,
judging the "pitiful convicts in chains,"
unable to free them like the ancients

on New Year's Eve. Afraid of losing
his government meal, he woke with the shame
of those in his charge. How is it a god of man

judges those with only leaves for tongues?
And stammering in their confusion,
what do they say that has not been broken

by tongues? They say nothing and listen
to the masters of the court, who today
found one worthy of his tongue,

his idea of being the sound of bells
that will ring in the small cathedral
of the voice made fully human.

When Jake Came Wheezing to the Door

bent with forty years of smoke and labor,
to ask directions to the Boar's Head Feast—

blew the words from his chest to begin
the doleful stare into us—"Good neighbors—
not like me, the asshole," his liver

halved by the pistol grip on a bottle
that might have sat dormant in a weaker hand—

this snow he walked to endure the shame
that will never be said. I coughed a stupid
"Come in," until he deferred, our porch

the chamber beyond what he could feign
in the silence between, there being no death

among friends, this day he knocked
a first hello in all our lives on this block,
the one we share like blood, now that he's left

but never really gone from the stones
of the street that turn a wintry hand within.

The Fallen Season

In the distance, a stream sings
in the rose hips—winter has stripped
its shores to icy prayers of green.

All the way from the hot springs
you mumbled words to pines—and did
they listen, encumber your burden

down the snowy road? On the porch
of sage, came the highest squeak—
a flycatcher weeping and then the wasp—

were they out of season? The hand
that loves the fallen wood broke twigs
and bulrushes to the stream, no path

to ford save rock and water in a gorge
of willow stems. I yelled when you fell
in the rose hips—and held the river wind,

waiting for a sign. Sun left the valley—
we sank the snowmelt to the house,
gathered bark and blew the night air

through the roof beams. An aging poet
lit the owlish sky of two beside the fire
and under them, crossed the lantern coals.

And then I let the ash go, tossed
in the bed until your skin set me down
to that cold water that runs between.

Letter to Ken in Farthest Logan

for Ken Brewer

I heard an owl come round the knees
but had no voice for the drumming, could say

nothing to the poet of mountains east and
the hoot would not go down: out of the salt flats

flew the bulk of feathers to a white ridge with a cabin
and the musk of books, where a man climbs the shelf to readers

to blur the owl and its offering, the blind wait for spring
below all buds shorn to stem, and like an orchid

of the night, the owl stirs the cabin once again—
no refuge here: the mind already swung to other heels

come round the door to nick and skin the shelves
that he might sing an anthem beyond the end.

Stacking Wood in Heavy Snow, Days Before Christmas

In this time of war
that will not console—
but could it be any other
                                        time—
there is no need
                        but forgiveness.

Far from my own small hand
            that condemns
dead wood to ash,
there is but dust
                        to divide—

but could it be a dust
                        of snow
            to summon the words
we could not speak—when, or if
            such beauty becomes
                        our world to share.

Daffodils One Sunday Before Snow

Already the bulbs croon
the silent damp,
the edge of spring
not days from here, land
of the thin green necks that sprout
before the last white morning—
because, of course, it will come.

Helpless in another silence,
my father-in-law stargazes
the iris of his eightieth spring,
asks for coffee to glaze
the reruns from the History Channel,
grunts at the goldfinch sock
he reminds is empty—

and having no earth,
angles his good leg to the door
where, in a fit of declaration,
lights a cigarette to defy spring,
to stand among the bulbs
however lithe his stem
this Lenten Sunday.

Running to Southern California

for my mother

Because the sycamore sky
is greased with rain and wind,
my mother steadies her house
for the return of family
from their destinations:
folk—kin—blood—beauty—
and whether we know our names
to be son or daughter
who rose from the green
and blue landscape
trimmed for the hands that bore us—
she stands, shaving onions
to enchiladas, the red sauce
dribbles to olives and avocado,
like dew in the trumpet flowers
out her window, the fallen
shoots of bottlebrush
on the tile, and when the prodigal
thrust is over,
she'll trace the orbit of us
alone on our roads,
in the comfort of dust.

What They Cannot Say Before Dark

There's lots to say that don't need words.
—Maxine Kumin

At the kiosk, thirteen women sit
their wheelchairs, trying to find a face.

The nursing station is empty, the light
blinks for assistance and the bell snickers

to no one. I walk in, cross their path
like a deer in the field of eyes but

they are true to the horizon of decline:
"How are you?" my mid-age attempt

at crossing over. A lean, gray woman
pivots in her podium—"We're not here—"

and suddenly excavates the history
of their chorus: this fragile band

of residents. I cannot answer her truth—
"Yes, you are," I trot like a magpie,

but we both know I am lying—and her
motif is the mercurial room of waiting:

for the volume to trail off, for the winter
to climb its icy fingers up the glass

and claim, not a voice, but a woman who,
without a perch, gave the group a name—

someone whose cognition disappears,
a sterile smile who turns the hall to bed.

On the Terraza

At last I am on the *terraza* with Lorca
before they outlawed wine and poetry—

at last, grape leaves and honeysuckle
descend from the clouds to the lips

of the fountain and the gypsy cat—
white and brown on the glass shards—

tickles the edge of *Calle del Rosal*
for birds or mice in the somnolent streets.

Too many months have crawled by without
the arrogant housefly at my nose,

the church bells on the occasional hour,
and the Moors peeking into a dream.

At last, at last, I sleep on the roof
of the Albayzín until the rising begins.

Every Day She Comes to Spain

for Mary O'Malley

Every day she comes through the dooryard
of cobblestones and white walls
to the piano in the grape leaves,

or the violin of bird wings in the fountain,
and aimlessly tugs the figs to ground
like nipples on the tethered dog—

all these fragrant episodes to save her,
like Machado's mistress on the roof
before death descended in rain

on this olive landscape, less a rose
than a bloom of one hundred years' color
in the canyons of the Albayzín. Last night

she phoned from Galway to soak
the Andalusian soil in her veins,
but I could not whisper its throated beauty

beyond these auburn hills to Malaga, and the ocean
between us, but she came, Moorish and mule-headed,
across the wire and it was breath enough

to labor with those who harrow by the sun
and its heraldic shadow: humbled,
opened to the *voluntud*—the will to go on,

dream a further dream of place without country,
the island below this angel of some other grace
she knows as love and dust on her tongue.

Los Vendedores

Out of the sand they come
crowing like cocks in the morning sun

chanting their strange, melodious hymns to food:
Tortillero, Helado, Maní tostado,

and the children, burnished and thin
scurry to meet the musical men

and the women, smoked in their shawls
float on brooms behind them

and the beach is never still
with the halo of hunger overhead.

Hunting for Rain

Walking your dog, Cookie,
through the low curbs of Carson,
wondering who will cash your check

for misery, for rain, so that you
might escape the brick terrace
of rent, of living outside this land—

the rucksack piled in your sled
when the cash burns through
and you stare at the night post

of stars, to ask if any blooded
creature will help, will dance
into your weekly motel to save

one more night from disgrace.
You insist the land is yours,
the car will start and the door will open.

To whom, I do not know—but to you,
black curls and fleece, it might be
Dorothy, the Tin Man, or the Lion

in the archway. It might be us
who try to sleep beneath those same
jagged stars. Even now, at the post office

with no key for your disability check,
the dog laps snow from steps,
and the rain down south washes its people

from the streets. I hope you make it, Maria—

to the candle in the church
outside of Chihuahua, Texas, or Tourmaline—

wasn't that the last place you visited,
with Cookie on his string and your sled
close behind, woman of the bone and arrow,

woman who must hunt soft eyes to eat.

September Light

In this time of whitened light
and aching wind from the west,

the spark of sage at my nose—
I return to my knees for strength.

I roved the Southwest, the red gorge
of Abiquiu and saw light unlike

any in the mooring of an eye. O'Keeffe
gave us these colors like thread.

Then wove the desert home—the rock,
the water, and the fossil of man.

Everywhere the sweet rot
of rusted cars on the road edge,

houses tumbled to sticks, and the pale
road sign smirking: *Come on in—hot food.*

In Tonopah we ate tortilla soup,
watched the miners swing at the big screen

prizefight on Saturday night. At long last,
we drove the wind-road to this house

where I learn from this light, now thirty-one
Septembers since the raven

cut a trail of wings on my back.
I have never known the desert

would be my answer. Still,
I listen for its arid question.

Heron Dance

I circled the river of blue necks,
their heads tipped like statuary, one white eye
driven to fish the stone pools until, stooped

for the hunt, the feathers lifted in flight,
crested the rocky points in midday heat
just yards from the bridge of man—

these twelve beaks parted the precipice and we
said nothing to the river riders, rolling beams of light,
pterodactyls that might be here tomorrow—

how things become they who cannot fly alone,
crucibles of hunger that wade and wade
to find reflection below the emerald blind

of the cut bank and I am not in their midst,
but in it still, water, that will by then bestow,
to those who so long from above, stare down.

Now I Sit the Saddle to Freedom

12:00 noon

Strangely wonderful it is
to bike this path
through eastern Arizona
without a belonging
to say my name.

5:30 p.m.

Crow at my back,
cattle in the creek meadow
and wildfire beyond the ridge—
is Snyder
still
in the lookout tower?

6:30 p.m.

Mountain bluebird,
buffalo, and perhaps
an angel below
the roadside cross—
her death came like rain.

8:30 p.m.

Sunset on the red-orange rocks—
so this is what Abbey saw.

A bike path leads to nowhere—
into the mouth
of Bryce Canyon,
a full moon rises.

Palliative

for Hayden Carruth

Are there words
for what you cannot,
lying in this wilderness, express—
with her hands to love you

to the center of the bed,
the window with a cardinal
at the lopsided feeder, and
the weathercock that crows

in all weather
as you almost crow
to the harrowing horizon
and the day after when solace

will be what we share
in the vowels of thirty books
left us to understand
our time was not misunderstood—

like you who wrote
whether in or out of mind—
the raging beauty of human arms
and took refuge there

just as we plunge them now:
nocturnal, redwing clarinetist,
hard-nosed master of the certain,
untimely trill before dawn.

What the Flower Might Say to Family

for the Ruiz-Gordons

Because there is no flower
for nine months in this northern land, and

because there are only florid towns
on the tin roof hillsides of the Costa Rican year, and

because there is no other earth or star
on which to post a son from the brown hills of home,

I weave between the father and mother
who took him into their green land—son of she

and I who could not forsake the journey to sage
and alkaline lakebed—what began as dust and dies

in his throat, the idea of desert
he forsook to embrace the florid ancestors—

the given sky of green damp, forest
of no name and a hundred names, and the last, *Naranjo*—

situated on the ridge of coffee and loss,
what this family became—the solace of something like fruit

for the son who knew scarce fruit,
this gathering of hands that climbed the tall one

and rendered his silence helpless, those we thank
with our stifled strength, four thousand miles north of green,

of day lilies cut from backyard stems, this warren
they dug to him—*familia*—the word, almost broken in

for these rueful months—and yet, we can break
no word for those who caught the lean one in their midst,

stood like bamboo to the son
who did not know fruit could be anything but dust.

Sunflower Ridge

So low your heads to the wind
of goldfinch and butterfly,

leaves like elephant ears
tip your stems to sun and follow

the harness of light from point
to compass point and why not

crawl such distance in the vacant sky
for the consumption of heat,

lean your one bone into what
you could not but feel

to synthesize carbon dioxide and water,
extract lemon from something like dust,

pitched to the universe
of ants and grasshoppers

like narwhals of no known origin,
the tridents of a lost ship

in the wings and fables
of a garden that spring set sail.

When a Poem Drew Its Breath in the Late Autumn of a Friday at Work

I

When the hourglass shifts to suffer
those I cannot comfort
with any skill of mind,

and the habitual retreat to shelter
seems the paradise we trade
for this beautiful wager of breath,

our tongues lanced in the cheap wine
of foundation talk
and board rooms of holy inquiry—

all this summons the artist
to rooms no one should have to visit,
this solemn imperfection, my life,

before I fish the wild eyes from my cranium,
the ones for whom regret
is an ordeal of handouts,

the last ingredients for a man
beating the treble clef of kill,
his wife on the phone somewhere

in the trailer, and I pretend
they don't exist, start the car
to put this day down, the razor

of daylight passed to dark again.

II

Yes, there in the razor light
kissing the ridge, my arm
          almost steady at the task, I raised

a small offering to the wild eyes
          no foundation will ever see,
the impertinent glass of poverty

that empties to this door
all the fantastic days of the year.
          I became translucent, smoked

in the diffidence that hails
          from desks like mine,
the radio darling alone in *Iraq, Iraq,*

and I gathered outside in the dark,
now nearly gone Friday
          of misunderstanding, and drove

to the sanctuary of dinner,
          that I ate like fool's gold
to wed the day over and skipped

to a sudden heaving sleep that could not
regard such time as peace—
          the kingdom we sleep for,

the art of imperfection,
          that cradles my lost words
in what was a longing to serve.

Letter to My Wife from the Coastal Plain, Arctic National Wildlife Refuge

You have lived with me longer than stone
with its unchosen mate of soil and there is no
perfect reason for this save your willingness
to be fractured by force greater than either
of us here in the last decades of our lives.

For five days I have sat riverside with
migratory birds and the first wild crocus
to risk its full height of one inch
before tonight's killing freeze. In the haze
of a quarter century's love for you,
I think no woman would rise from rock

to make her purple wings felt on this
June day—but of course, you have, and
have again, to save me with petals that
otherwise would fall to the grave descent
of lying alone in this valley of arctic water.
When I wake from winter cold it is like

the resurrection of field grass
in this raw place without you, and I am
steadied by your resolve to return
to the unborn field of my brown hands,
witness to the morning you broke from earth
the rooted shadow of what I was.

From *Snowmelt* (1994)

Snowmelt

for Jess Hayashi

I came for an evening and a day
of fishing. I caught Jeffrey pines
arched in the Shasta sky
and the rage of water from the boat,
snowmelt, in the silver mouth
  of a stream.

Your eyes were so rich and brown
as you held the smallmouth bass in your hand
and pronounced, "All bones, nothing to eat,"
then flung her over the tip of your rod
to the chill green water below.
A splash and it was gone.

The flutter of a minnow
kept the four-pound test alive
till the snap of a rainbow
brought you over the bow.
The reel shed line
with each quiver of the hook,
but you worked that trout to the end.

We cleaned the fish on the bulkhead
at Salt Creek. The pilings from the pier
rose like splinters in the water; they warmed
more darkness than I care to tell.

All the Worthwhile Things

are in bed, swirling
above my good friend's head
in a vase of roses
she nightly gives to me
with the awkward satisfaction
of a flower girl at a wedding.

Always, I play down her dreams
knowing the wind nearly howled
me to death last night; she only
stirred, slipped somewhere
beneath the covers
as a sand dollar
might slip beneath the sea.

I awoke to find the porch
curiously strewn with leaves
and paper—all the clutter
of a high desert storm. She drank
coffee on the steps,
knowing also I would sweep them
then sit beside her warm brown legs
for want of a fire.

We shoveled little pools
in the earth where our toes
could rest, and waited for
the sun to awaken speech.
At last, I realized there was none:
she was alone and dreaming
peacefully about the roses.
And I? I was beside her
dreaming of us.

On Highway 50

The loneliest road in America
—Life Magazine

She lies on a plain of sagebrush
and chipped blue asphalt
making its way
to the nowhere edge of Nevada.
I drive this road and she

crawls to the periphery
of my vision
as if she were looking
for someone to speak with.
I feel empty

at the turnout on Highway 50.
The railroad sign
stirs in the wind
and some unknown offspring
of the desert says, "No,

don't leave me.
I have waited with the sand
in my mouth for years
and still I am no more
than a thread of desire."

A Place of Stone

for Ben and Karen

I come for the wooded dance of the Comstock:
the piñon pine, harsh as the face of an owl;
juniper, a scruff beard on the high desert;
and locust, spent, with purr of cicadas.

I come alone, in a blue-black forest of night,
steal my way into the folds of darkness,
risk ruin under the light of a star. I come
as so many others must, for that which is missing
from the stencil of the city: the outline of a face
on the back of a horse, the quiet rocks
that grow and grow in the sun's burnt strokes,
and the pine nuts glazed with sap in fall.

I come for the fissures that ripple through this land:
the empty spell of a mine shaft, water
dripping in like a slow clock from above;
the breaking, the chipping, the bloody salt smells
that ride the canyons. A trail of ashen dreams
flake the golden skin of Nevada.

I come to fill the fallow contours of my mind
with a place of stone, yet nearly everything
has been stripped from these slopes.
Even the cornflowers cower in the tailings.
Cattle graze on winter roots, and a farmer
fingers heat from the stove.
Fences crawl over half-bleached plains,
touch the moon's corrosive light

and I return, a wisp of desert wood.

In a Sparse Tone

for Richard Shelton

In the quiet areas
where speech will never come
I hear your footsteps
reaching out on the dry
Sonoran wind, making those
desperate desert sounds
that one must make
to survive where the sun
and the sand meet
like two parched lips
on the horizon.

I wonder then, if
it isn't you, dear Richard,
who is weeping
over the warm apricot earth
quietly filling your
freckled hands with tiny
pools of melancholy
or concern, or just plain fear
that nothing will ever
grow to enchant you
like the playful path

of a desert creek gone dry.

On the San Francisco Zephyr

A diesel dons its black plume,
fences grate at the dust.
This train rides through backyards.
Scrap metal and glass
twist along the tracks;
boxcars bent on siding grass.

The passengers read
like a menu: hot, bland, or broken.
I return to the prattle
of a book on blue roads. Sun
dangles fingers in my scalp,
deadens the insistent clatter

of steel. Faces turn to wheels,
roll me back
to the icy edge of Nevada.
For so little, I would travel
your desolate arteries
to the end, but oh, America

the rails slap beneath me
and I cannot find a pulse.

Thien Hong*

for V. N.

The sun rises in black circles
above a silver roof and plywood walls.
He touches the skin of each child
as if they were flowers, waits for breath
to stir dreams from their heads.

The kitchen fills with steam,
green tea kindles their spry limbs.
She kneads the flesh of the youngest,
his bones a frail tribute
to the camp he was born in.

He peels the sheet from the window frame,
the clatter of children muffle
a barbed vision of water's edge.
It tears through light like
a seam to the world outside.

The car bursts forth with a blue cloud.
Faces huddle in back. Wiper blades strip dew
from glass. She brings it to a stop;
his eyes are dark as coal. He shouts
"Goodbye!" The others crawl out at schools

drawn gray and damp from age. In class
she studies the crooked rules of syntax;
her voice flush with desire
from a stolen land. At work,
her husband crowds a file room desk,

pages the still life of numbers
in pink and yellow stacks.

* red sky

When his boss yells, he recoils:
the mouths rise up from the ashen floor
of memory, anger clots his throat.

“You could feed them for six weeks—”
a co-worker’s admonition spins
at the base of his neck. Rings
coil about him, throb lower back
where caged, they kicked for seven years.

Her words come softly to him:
“Without you, we have no one.”
On break, he sips coffee with cream,
presses the limits of language:
“I learn Latin as a boy, speak French,

teach math—, route purchase orders—”
At preschool, she catches the small face.
He splashes sand on the tires,
climbs to her arms. They journey home,
ginger teems with chicken. The two bedrooms

are quiet; the boy sleeps, she reads
from a notebook. The lines blur
with phrases. Her tongue turns upward,
splits sound as it crests the palate,
blooms, and slides to the floor.

Her eldest daughter feeds the washer
as it bobs in dark clay.
The machine dances against sheetrock.
Tomatoes, peppers, and parsley
crowd the damp borders of trees.

Sun filters in the basement,
invoices come to a clean, sorted stop.

Manila folders climb shelves to the ceiling.
He gathers lunch sack, overshirt,
and plies the pavement to a familiar link fence.

Shouts pour from the house.
At the door, he holds her thin arms,
turns, settles to a chill beer.
A game show rankles from a swollen nightstand,
the boys fight like jackals at his feet.

The youngest crawls to his chest,
lifts the bulky glasses overhead.
She scuttles a towel at the waist,
they sit below a cross on the mantle.
The sheet comes down the window.

Fog spills in from the bay.
A faint cry from the back room,
he whispers to a small face, tracks the wood
to bed. She sleeps without notice;
he finds breath at his side.

Woman Empty

On her heart
a growth flames
with hatred.
In a room, numb with men,
she is too weak
for the stench of passion.

They want more
than tented thighs
and pearl skin. Hard hands
rake a bed of coals;
breathe the blood
of her legs.

The seed spins like rice
at her waist.
She screams for the face
of a friend;
they rack flesh
with fingers of stone.

In December Steam

in memory of John Lennon

December 8, 1986

Six years ago today, beneath the iron gate of the Dakota,
you fell from the world. Made lead
by the hands of a psychotic fan, gun more surreal
than candles on the sewer grate. All night,
the irrational chorus of voices, chanting
"All we are saying—"

New York, an anonymity on the Upper West Side:
the clouds of protest gone from the street.
A song drifts like a humid wind and you
are riding the crest of a lyric more painful
than the tears we broke for you. We reel
from the rhythm, our psyche blind at the altar.

Sacrifice, the window through which you spoke,
your playful stroll in December steam
transfixed on a vision of peace. Imagine war
gone from our lives! hunger and greed,
a levee spilled over. Singing the dream
of one flesh, you walked in this world.

A raven boy called out, "Father."
Fallen bird, you touched his wings.
The woman, so dark in her repose, kindled heart
in your eyes. Flush with family, the sound
was hopeful. At forty, a fantasy
for the radio waves. And we nearly let go—

but nothing prepared us for your passing
save the riddled speech of a bent subway rider.

While Stones Rage

At the Vietnam Veterans Memorial,
Washington, D.C.

Pencils arc the names of the deceased,
release them from the terror of black stone.
In the lexicon of war, letters dance:
no sound in the lives that perch
among the newsprint, the aging metal stars.

Vietnam! a noun that will not die;
silk work in the minds of a generation:
remorse lies furrowed in marble lines
that flower among street vendors
and limestone walls beyond.

Fervent the settling rock, patched into earth,
treated, retreated like nausea from afar.
Nothing disturbs the quiet language of fear;
it reels on, the horror of young men,
minds gone to the garden of red light.

On the horizon, a bloated rucksack
in the rain forest of verb to be. Fresh names
soothe the spring of honor;
stones rage in the memory
of short lives, guns muted in wonder.

The Contours of Travel

Mosquito, fat with my blood—
you pierce flesh
with a thin, brown needle,
thrash ankles with vile antigen.
Each day, a new red clot
festers beneath damp skin.
I measure your fired presence
with wings at my feet.

Equatorial land:
green, glowing green!
rain spilt to a heated floor.
The bites swell to a warm blue.
Fluid cracks from a pore;
flecks of sand
tease its beaded flow,
white cells stream in.

I page a pale book
through light unfiltered.
You etch and infect as I rest
to a great scroll of sky.
A cartographer of pulse and marrow—
you must fly, dear lady,
to be weighted by blood.
Come script the arch and heel.

Face of Light

for E. L.

She sleeps alone for comfort;
no one can hold her—not I
nor the doctors, nor the shrewd minds
of science. Not one to calm the muscles
that rattle flesh to dawn.

Her shrill cry lashes out
like a woman in labor.
And what to make of the stars?
such bright signs on a canvas
colored with moonlight—

The ritual of longing for daybreak
is over; she rests in shaded light.
Moments drift to morning,
flush adrenalin through her veins
and soon, the hands return

for pulse, fluid, or pressure,
and inevitably turn away
to meter progress on a chart.
She pulls at the curtains
that shroud her existence

day after receding day and colors the room
with sun. If not for her vision
of a tranquil flesh, not one
could rise to still
the faint marks of its passing.

Social Work

I cannot shake their faces.
They clamor through a sleepless night.
For so long, the shards of voices—
even as I draw closer to the edge.

Their lives are blistered
with children, bad checks,
and pain-killing hatred
for the one that got them there.

And I, a feeling-stone
for those who must lay
down their emotions
in the sterile comfort of an office.

They form lines
long before I arrive,
chart the path that separates
from job, home, or spouse.

If it ended there, if
I could thwart their anger
with the crude tools of this profession,
if I could turn from the vile

fragments of their speech,
if I could return the frail volley—
if it ended there,
I would cry at day's end.

PORTRAIT OF A LADY

for deborah

soft
would have been
the sound i heard

slight
the color
i saw seep in the room

wan
the eyes
that watched me move

sweet
the lips
pressed on my tongue

smooth
the arms
pulled to my chest

still
the thoughts
that crept across your face

slow
the smile
that swayed before me

sunlight
between us
on that first fragile morning

Baja California Sur

for D. and S.

I

I finish a full moon
on the Sea of Cortés.
Waves break
like wet lips,
brush silence
between people. At dawn
we tear clams from the reef
in a village no larger
than us.

You and I
have traveled to the end
of this peninsula
in search of a warm
Spanish sun, and now we are
with the saguaro, succulent
of the Sierra Madre,
and the lava flows
that drift so darkly to water.

The most we can hope for is wind;
at the very least
salted air
from the round stretch of sea.
What moisture to be had
is driven through sand
and even that, my friend,
is spoken for. At land's edge
we are pitched in the ruin of stones.

II

We have brought our love
to be nourished
by the earthen roads and
clapboard cantinas,
to move among the cattle and lone
switch of snake;

have come to heal
our feeling for each other
even as the waves
crack still more shells
on the rocks below.

We come unfinished
as only one can,
to pretend
for these few days
that love is a soft orange sky
and you and I
its clouded followers.

We come to forget
that our lives
have been kept like linens
in a smooth brown chest
and that before long
the labor of living alone
will set in
and our skin will go
from blue to gray.

III

There is no need to hide
from flesh.
It is only
the unnatural stillness
of life without you
I fear.

If we should retrace steps,
let it be you and I
who touch skin
to the waves.
If we should hear their crack,
let it be on petals of sand
spun in the dry salt wind
that we fall.

And if, after the cold
quiver of years,
we should return
to this jagged place,
let it be for a white string moon
or a clean summer rain.
Let the saguaro streak the earth
with green limbs,
and let us break down
and be broken into.

Father's Coral Heart

I

Raven boy holds her picture
at his fingertips.
Ash drops
on the border soil
of National City.
He grazes the hood,
jump-starts a '39 Ford
throttles the road to Mexico,
snaps every rule
like a sailor on leave.
Lights, dim as the moon
at dawn; her face
deep in the folds
of leather.

II

On his break
fingers dance on Formica top.
A slide rule
splits the tension
of chemistry and rent,
bowling pins
hung by hand. Mother
teaches school; books
are loose in the kitchen.
A child turns
the Irish light in his eyes.

III

In windless heat
of garage, sweat
layered beneath his glasses,
chisel steadied
between thumb and forefinger,
he stoops over wood lathe,
crawls down the spine
of a dowel. The mahogany
spits curls of sawdust
up his forearms.
He smiles:
the plug firmly planted—
a desk, knotted for life.

IV

Headstrong
at a steel desk,
fingers pinched like wire
on a circuit board,
he descends
into language of resistors.
Nothing to capture
the gentle twitch
of equations
save fresh green lines
on sketch paper.
A slim, white face
recedes, the veil
of corporate science.

V

A father
mired in middle age,
lashed to family
by what he was.
He fingers the stairs
in beveled darkness.
Children linger
in front room portrait,
like vines from the hearth.
He pieces, ever pieces
chambers together,
the ritual
of speechless ways.
His heart,
a great humidor
for kith and kin.

VI

A sailor
stretched over the bilge,
diesel in the grease
beneath his nails,
eyes brighter
than a jetty light in fog.
His face, warmed to a red
sky; nothing
to peel the moon away.
On the fly bridge,
he crests five-foot waves,
cackles for the gulls. She
sands teak on her water house;
lives tarnish with sun.

VII

Grandfather glistens
with his plump, blond boy.
The wagon jerks
with ten fat fingers,
bumps down unpaved street.
Mother scatters dust from the porch.
He presses the moist skin
to his cheek,
whisper of new breath.

The life shed
that morning she moved:
hood, leather, and ash,
faintly dress
his amber face.

To My Son

I will never feel you at my breast
as your mother feels you now.
Perhaps I will learn
the hungry ways of your mouth,
but for this moment, I must listen
to your whisper in her arms.

You have crept
into the warm speech of my sleep,
and like so many fathers before me,
I make way for the tears
you speak to me
in the pearled darkness of the evening.

And when movements in your flesh
begin to wake you,
we watch the first cracks of light
as they spill over our hair and skin,
and you, the writhing one,
reach to catch them
as they move across my face.

You catch my lips instead,
and I tell you that even now
at just six weeks
I cannot bear your absence.
I have come to rely
on the wind from your lips
as though it were flesh touching mine.
You shake me and I am reminded;
this is who you are:
this is how you move away from the womb

and follow the lines across our faces
to a life of your own, my son.

Married Student Housing

At dusk, the scratch of squirrel's feet.
Later still, the erratic shift of keys
linger in this cinderblock flat.
The two of us, bare in this place,
mark days with letters from friends.
We share voices soiled with reason,
tire among the endless sounds,
and lay our son upon us
in the plum light before dawn.

You and I travel these sterile rooms
like brother and sister.
The table is where you write;
I eat there and edit your lines.
We came here for an education.
We have received life without life
in the delicate hands of the learned.
Few expect us to return
short of breath and purpose.

Perhaps they are right. We have left
ourselves in three short years
and we will leave even more
at its conclusion. These things tread on;
another family will displace us
with their desire to learn.
And then we are reminded: we sleep
with the supple pounding of squirrels.
The walls are pale flesh now;

soon they will be brittle and faint,
a memory, skillfully dying among us.

Watch Him Walk

Walking out this morning with your
blond hair buried in a down vest
and the sky so gray we could touch it,
it was hard letting you go,
harder still watching
you tremble your way across
those broken orange leaves,
threading that thin line of balance
like you were being pulled away from me.

How is it you make your steps
so soft and unsure, wavering
all the while with those feet
barely large enough to hold you,
arms spinning like leaves from a tree
and your smile thicker than bluegrass?
You fairly made me cry,
slicing the air with your life
so small. Oh my son, where
did you learn to walk like that?

If You Are Unable

to gather
any further
hue and cry
look not within
but remark
that it has passed
and journey
simply, home.

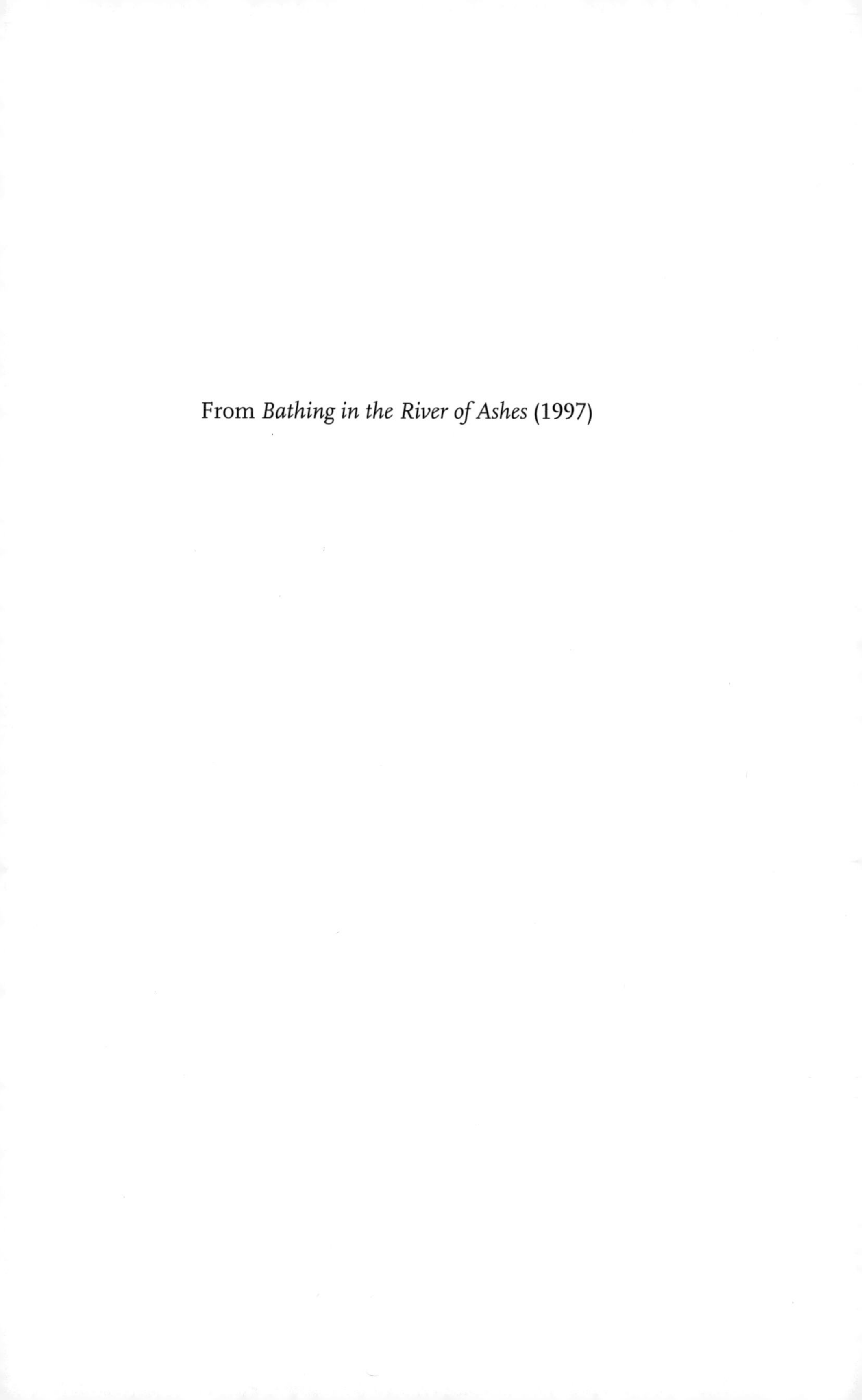

From *Bathing in the River of Ashes* (1997)

After Lunch at the Blueberry Cafe: Las Vegas, 1994

for Stephen Shu-Ning Liu

Soon the Strip will flame
with neon, and no tourist
will return as he came
to the aboriginal soil
that crowds to dust where

patio lawns and weathered
magpies spar for water
or any ghost of moisture
in the momentary desert
this late spring day.

At the substation I finger
Walter Clark's trembling leaves
and wonder what rogue seed
choked to birth them
on this six-lane highway.

But I cannot walk this sand like a city,
only the wells of sadness
that lie in pockets of overturned sky
and the few wild things left
to mark my journey south—yellow flowers

pitchforked with ants
on a creosote bush. Whose home
this dusted prairie we paved
for pleasure? Whose home
do we squirrel away to now?

Hawthorne

for Gary Short

In a town where bombs
buy a day's work and bunkers
blight the desert like bones,
how happy can you be
straddling a stool at El Capitán
with the windows coiled in smoke
and the jukebox jarring K-9
through the reeds of country soul?

The casino fades to lavender
shoulders on Highway 95.
Tourists brake to read "Danger—
Low Flying Aircraft, Do Not Stop,"
and the hangars climb to the sky
and detours swallow transport trucks
bound for Reno or beyond.

And still the bunkers lie, mouths open
like barrels in the rain.

The Cliff House Saloon, quiet as fog,
boasts "Armed Forces Day—
Proud to Serve You," and the old ones
wait for the second Tuesday in July
when the hydroplanes
light up Walker Lake.
Even it looks flatter than it should.

The children play on decommissioned
three-inch, fifty-caliber anti-aircraft guns
as if they were powder blue
dinosaurs in Ladybird Park,

thinking, how much better can it get?
In a once-mighty high school
seniors graduate to thieve from Mormon sky.

And bunkers die in peacetime.

The barracks are nearly closed now.
The moon rises in sills of solitude
and the last drunk shuffles from
Joe's Tavern like a cloud
come to rescue this swollen town.
And the wind moves like a skirt
through the clapboard siding
beached in stones at her feet.

The Meyer Cabin, Jarbidge

What holy thread made man come down this road?
To this sovereign stable, chinked with mud,
animal fat, and barrel staves,
a stream-fed backwoods cabin high
in the wedge of wilderness the first
federal survey team cut from Nevada, sloped
to nearly forty acres, and if you include the Diamond A,
broken as it is from the world, island after island
of land atop the river gorges, it may as well be
another country, out here in the vacant
West old Abbey bore, bookless, looking

for a hand, and he knew then the song
was wild and migratory like birds,
coming here dusted as planks, peeled
from the road of forty-seven miles in, good God
was it Jarbidge held in the black wake of fire
summer last, and storm-sweet Monday in July,
unpredictable pee-pot, cantankerous valley,
have I finally wept this womb of cold earth
and left it to seethe in the bedspring air
some tall cloudless day in a crooked house come down
to fiddle our lives in this small fork of creation?

At the Old Santa Fe Club in Goldfield

The Sundog Bed and Breakfast sign
squeaks like an iron saddle in the wind.
Even the diesels downshifting at the curve
slowly fade. Gravel rings the schoolyard
in a rosary for better times, and kids climb the poles
that anchor double-wides to the ground.

"Gold went down and they say the Test Site is going
to New Mexico in '91. Bad management, I guess."

Out here, rumors and books, like all quiet things,
blow through the cracks of moon and sun
where people sit thankful for their coming.

"You serve food?" I ask.

"No, not much here since the mine closed.
Be like everything else, I guess—
they'll wait till there's a foot-a-snow and it's colder
'n-a-bear's ass to open it again. The Mozart Club
is the only one serving food anymore."

Game One of the World Series tonight.
She tilts the ash from her cigarette and says,
"Land's going down, like everything else, I guess."

If the Greyhound stops at all, it will be
the driver who steps off for coffee or Don's Donuts
trucked in from Tonopah. Later, at the Gables
there's crazy chatter in the cellar,
shadows growing on the family plot, and
nothing but rust to take them from here.

NEVADA NO LONGER

> This is a case in which the public
> has to trust the scientists.
> —Tony Buono,
> USGS Hydrologist,
> Nevada Test Site

Nevada is never on the map, not now,
not ever.
                    If only
I could finger a word
for the few who live
                              by the sun,
what would it be: itinerant,
sparse, dragon people
                              who fly
in the sand and spin before the books
that name a cactus to clothe
the loins of uranium down deep?

No, it would not be harsh; rather
we live here.
We raise family, split wood,
shovel snow, and read of our absence.

Nevada is never on the map
not now, not ever,
                              save the day
a green lung percolates
from two miles below volcanic tuff—
then you will recognize us
as the place that kills
or was killed, but for now
I cannot find a way down Alternate 95—
not scholarly, not radical, not
known. And still, faces cling

to the taverns of Beatty,
Tonopah, and Yerington.

Where do I go to lie with the yucca? California?
No, it is many things but quiet.
Oregon? No, it is wet and
dry there, so I remain
home
with states before and aft
coming like insects
to the Test Site, coming
with something to read.

Today, I tell my son
of a desert with no name. He remarks
"Why?" I do not know—Nevada is
never on the map, not now
not ever.

On the Death of the Culture Dog, Nevada's Last Bookstore

I pull the solitary handle—not another slot—
and know the smell of something fine
gathered for posterity: William Everson's poems
the fifth of fifty, signed, handmade by Capra Press.
A final volume of recollections by Miller,
and further still, Shakespeare aging
in a china cabinet. Somewhere in the lost
temple of the desert, these few have made a
forest, book-like, of belief in things rare
and old. Belief that cannot be copied:
a remarkable feat where tourists play
in the change girl's hand. Even the paint
on the building is the color of
                                        sand at sunset.

The message comes in bold letters: *40% OFF!*
Going out of business June 12—and
turn to take my swipes at a shelf.
Who will it be this fertile time?
Merwin, Paz, Bishop, or Wright—
I cannot take them all. No
money will buy these friends. They will
return to Bronx warehouses and bitter the columns
of bean-counters in high-rise offices. Good
for them, I think, let the bastards burn
                                        poetry for heat in Manhattan.

                                But we live in the desert,
somehow richer for a stretch of sun.
We will carry on without literature for trade
but not like it. Come back, Culture Dog,
we are churchless with your leaving. There is no place
to footnote a loss in the bookstore granaries
                                        of America.

First Cast, Late December, Pyramid Lake

for Jess Hayashi, 1951-1991

Today, fly-fishing the algaled dark
of Pyramid, snowstorm at my back,
I heard you in the mud hens, crying

when the cutthroat snapped the leader,
pink mouth opened to saline water,
it was you who swallowed,

bore the wooly worm in your maw,
my gloved forefinger pressed to cork
and the fluorescent line stiff in silver tow.

We floated the silted bed, squirmed
the Pleistocene floor, then calm in waders
you mocked California gulls from the nets,

plunged coots in the tufa. "Worthless bird,"
you said on our last visit with full, steamed
breath, then swore stalking in the wind,

ladder lapping the shore. Brittle man,
I can never catch the friend you were,
but I will fish to the end.

And when my rod buckles,
I will know it is you who bites
and boldly spins the reel at my palm.

Magpie Funeral

My scavenger husband picked you
from pavement, drove the eight miles
up the grade, found a telephone spool
off the porch, and waited for flesh to dry.

Black-billed to scruff the desert,
he wanted you for the alligator headdress
on his flatbed Chevy. But when the breath
of twenty birds came solemn from the locusts,
we knew it was more than carrion on the circular table.

Robed in black and white, they swooped
one at a time to the wooden altar.
For over an hour, their hushed flight
echoed the loss of a crow dancer
with the last dry speech of family.

Each bird, dressed in shadow, came
without calling, without invitation,
touched kin to understand:
scavenger, you can eat no more.

Never satiated, they flew to scour
what little breath had settled
in the hollow of your craving,
leaving you with wings spread,
oh bird of prey, as if to reach sky.

They Go Gathering Pine Nuts

Out there on the grade,
brittle as a couple of rain gutters
they stoop to misbehave: cussing,
cantankerous, stuck in the craw of cones,
it's nearly a holiday from the wifely
flatulence of home, festering with sap
Buddy and Hal, grumble in suspenders:

"They're too damn small—"

"They're what we get—"

gristly like an old married couple
they toss the broken ones to the ground.
A Paiute ghost slows a breath of wind
and still they burst with thumbs,
bootlegged and haggard, to strip the piñon.
Saddled in sun at midday, caught
between needle and stone, they knock shins

to tailgate and paddle through the ugly
tales that collar round their mountain
before the growling stiffness sets in and
they retrieve the burlap bags to slide
the Dodge to town, boil and dry
the wooden shells that yearly drop
to feed the restless boys again.

First and Last Things

for C., on being released from prison

The sun rose to part steel. Today
you stepped from that place
where they kept you cold and dark
as anthracite coal, walked twenty feet
from the yard that burns men down,
and gave your last goodbye to

the aluminum tray they fed you on
the photo with number pigeoned below
the blue cotton sweat gathered under you arms
the six a.m. count cleared before you,

frozen in the rails of feeling, walked not
ten feet to hear the bars barrel
down to the scratch of hoes on the warden's lawn.

And though it was your last day
you managed to look back and befriend
a face full of memories so bleak
even your eyes could not hold them.

Then, like a cloud breaking,
you
stepped through the gate of our house
and for the first time in eleven-and-a-half years

climbed stairs, sniffed blue spruce,
ran fingers through golden retriever,
touched sparkling cider to tongue,
crossed asphalt laid for all to travel,
breathed sky, and bore no sadness
when you saw sixty miles of mountain

and valley and said, "I want you
to write this down: *Now those years
are gone to dreams."* My son ran
balloons through your arms
and you burst into color
like the fingers of crocus at your feet.

Then you ate for the first time
breakfast on legs of maple and hand-painted plates
so pink and yellow I think you gave up eating altogether
and sat shining before the cactus given you
for the journey home.

La Desterrada

for Emma Sepúlveda

Woman without soil
you carve roots
from the stones of this town
and wander, if ever you can,
among the cowboys, call girls, and
neon of the North.

So many faces
held in your hands:
you quilt the fabric
of their lives
in black and white,
silence that must be sung.

Child of Chile,
you left the fear of hiding
and now, two decades gone,
you long to close
the dream of life in a land
without exile.

Melancholy believer,
come finish the dark
days of your youth
on this snow-capped
stone place
of our meeting.

Un moreno en la cocina

no tiene ojos
ni manos
solo una cara
que lleva platos al horno
hasta un lugar cerca de los tenedores
y regresa para nadar
entre las ollas. No conoce
los que comen afuera
los que limpian sus labios
bajo las cucharas y cuchillas
y salen por la puerta
con las manos derechas. Todo el mundo
come así: sin razón
antes del día para salir
cuando el sol baja en los ojos
del moreno que lava los vasos
sobre la memoria de la familia caen
de maíz, de coyote, desde
                                        el ferrocarril
subiendo la cocina de piedra hasta la casa.

A Brown Man in the Kitchen

has no eyes
nor hands,
only a face
that brings plates to the oven
to a place close to the forks
and returns to swim
among the pots. He does not know
those who eat outside,
those who clean their lips
on spoons and knives
and leave for the door
with right hands. All the world
eats like this: without reason
before the day to leave
when the sun goes down in the eyes
of a brown man who cleans glasses
over the memory of family, fallen
from corn, from coyote, from
                                        the railroad
climbing from the stone kitchen of home.

This Is Not Love's Offering

for a child in the Sudan

Having little to do with Eros
the vulture cranes to feed:
the child of famine recedes
to skin, and the black bird inches
to pierce the web of pulse
playing out on the desert floor.

The bird may not know
the breath of a child, may
be unfamiliar with his sighing.
But soon the two will merge
to prey upon the living
in a photograph.

When the child wakes
to another world, solemn
with the feathers of struggle,
there will be no eyes to receive him,
no camera to record. He will lie
as he was, in the kingdom of birds.

"Seems I'm All I've Got Anymore"

She side-stepped the lifeless
flesh of a stroke into the office,
dangled limbs like ice cream,

and managed the words, "I can do this job!"
her voice a sparrow
caught in a fireplace flue.

With no angels to redeem
she begged for a chance
to move in a room of machines.

And they let her perform a function.
Soon the troubled messages flew:
"Who called? I can't read this!"

With her right wrist she scissored manila
folders on the paper cutter and with her left
worked the halves to the ruler's edge,

having been cut to half-time, her interviews
sliced the long story that trails flesh,
and gathering all the scraps of paper,

she shuffled to the door, mumbling the curious
side effect of living in a full-flesh world:
"I don't know what's going to become of me ..."

Madonna in Traffic

Your eyes, shunted away in dark
amniotic fluid, what do you see
staring onto Boulder Highway,
mother straddling the island with cars
slipping either side of her waist,
what face do you look upon
stringing headlight to tail with the
unknown family at the intersection?

Her sign is finger-painted with magenta
letters but you cannot read the words.
Hungry. Pregnant. Need Work. Help Please.
You must not know her ringless stranger
as she coughs the cardboard high into the air
then stills your limbs, swinging into the flesh
you now gather. For seven months
you have trailed jobs to cities hot and broken

and once there, the old streets and soda crackers
came easy but inside the cotton dress
that blows toward Lake Mead, you wonder
if the next exit will find the hot meal
promised in long-ago Kansas, or shots
mother missed hitching out here. This road
has grown like a child and nothing, not traffic,
not plain people will shade the world outside,

but this small face that crowds her skin,
this membrane she touches
with stomach to sign may as well be
her breathing room where it's calm and smooth
and that's how you feel the fetal drum
looking out on this six-lane highway
with all Las Vegas glowing in the mirror
of every timid glance driving home from work.

Visiting Day

for C. and A.

I watch the tulips rise from the ground
like stones from this ashen place
and the bare wires of rose, shining thin,
thorns for the days that drift
to years, each green spike
spent on this March, March morning.

Snow broke my sleep at dawn.
And now the prison barbs
coiled in the ice—who will touch them?
or say "We are the men who dare
to crawl home from this place." My friend wants
to sleep outside—the cold cannot

change his mind. His face, softened now
by a woman—spare and loving.
Like others here, they retreat to touch
in this blue, smoky room. The guards pace
like ratchets in a clock. "Campers," they cry out.
Four men rise from the couch
like denim clouds

who must return—as we all must
to our caged rooms—to sleep with fire
even as snow pools white
on the concrete sky.

The Somali Cab Driver Tells of Ethnic Cleansing: Hart Senate Building, Washington, D.C.

He drives in the mirror:

"You a lawyer or a lobbyist?"

No. I work alone.

"You want something?"

Yeah, what about you?

"When I came to this country
I worked in the Somali Embassy.
They began thinning the population.
They knew where to find me."

You started driving a cab?

"Four hard years. I go to Howard.
The best black college in the country.
It's bad out there but I can do it.
We are fifteen—family in the Sudan,
Toronto, and North America."

And if you leave?

"In Africa there are 53 to 54 countries—
three are democratic. The rest
kill what they do not like."

You better let me out here.

And the black heart of Africa
is dying in D.C. cabbies
fallen from their home.

At the River's Edge

Montgomery, Alabama

Down here at the confluence of the Coosa
and Talapoosa, the Alabama winds brown
through the red clay of this southern city,
you can fairly smell the blood wedged in the banks
of this great river spilling its way to Mobile.

Today, James Meredith joined hands with Jesse Helms
to unearth the southern cross, and we in the West
look on smugly without a trace of water to defend.
Where now does the river run, with so few
to feel the anguish of its claws? But I stand here,
Alabama, and make words like
bowls to hold you, to hold you in my arms.

And though they will not do, you run through me,
make silt out of my eyes. I come back a log
bloated on your brown belly and float
the three hundred miles to sea, your skies so full
of rain they cry for the bones
that bevel darkness beneath my feet.
Down here where the river runs free and cold to the sea.

BLACK ENGLISH VERNACULAR

found poem from a text on
black speech and its interpretation

he home; we happy
he be late
we be there
they was early

john work yesterday
he work every day
they works downtown
he done his work on time

we ain't got no coffee nowhere

he done lived there for years
he be dead now
he home, we happy

Until They Come Home

for Levi and Rachel

After the police took the Biblical names given you,
scoured arms and backs for clues, we the nameless in your wake
knew there were words you will never touch again:
monster, the black headdress he wore
stalking dark the trailer window
who bore small fear in the whole of you,
and now the worm of boyfriend's failed hate
sleeps alone in a crowded cell.

As we drove to the thrift store,
hunger gathered in your mouths like rain
till Levi burst out, *"Milk!"* and held
the cold white to his lips and drank it all.
Then the quick slap of another word: *belt,*
black with silver studs poking from its leather core.
What stories did he bury in the throats of you,
hair curled for a month of Sundays?

Once inside, the two of you rocked the hangers
for pants, dress, sweater, shoes—with no laces for her, no—
and a word came: *stun gun.* I held her foot: *"Not if I tie them tight,*
he won't do it again." Rachel, you dressed for more than church,
purged aisle after aisle till the blue and red skirt
matched all but the most seasoned of surrogate shoppers.
The cashier blinked at the familiar scurry
of hands clothed at last.

Outside the sun crested west and we fed again,
small faces who seemed to eat all day. At the Carson Plains Market
Friday paychecks dribbled in, but mother, late in a lost car,
feared the worst. No doctor, no father,
"Where have you taken my children?" We passed the hours

hearing of old homes broken with family stones
and knew no God would rise to still the coyote's
listless cry come from the cold ridge beyond.

When the stubble of Ford finally slowed and she poured out,
black hair a snarl of pain and tired worry, kids running
screaming, *"Mom, Mom!"* I knew there was no home,
no safe place that would ever give shelter from the desert,
only a trailer floor filled with socks and stories
of how it used to be, before poor, before this new man
came wild through the door to make graves
of two so small as you.

Those People

Those people on the street
soiled with the grain of hunger
and thrift store bins, those people
lying next to you on cold red bricks
go to work, break bread, and eat
in the plum stairwell of Reno's dry lights.

Those people dream darkness will slip
from the fingers of their children
and the shelter will stay open one more night.
Those people, hardened in the rafters
of downtown lines, hand their best smiles
to soup kitchen chefs every morning,
drown hope in foolish talk of California,
bus rides, and relatives that curl with each passing day.

Those people lying next to you
wear my shoes, your hat, and no name.
Come, let us breathe the steam table
smoking in their eyes.
If mercy can be shown,
let us not forget the place-keepers
addled with keys and coffers,
who collect small dreams from children—
football, cribbage, and rag dolls,

we who deduct those people in food bank ledgers,
and still they blow like ice into our lives.

Bathing in the River of Ashes

The next time we meet, any of us, it will be
on the ashes of all that we once cherished.
—Henry Miller

Four women wash coffee skin. A *tikka* on the brow.
Children bob in a river of white and brown.
On either side of the gorge, Shiva and Bissnu swim in the grass.
The Dying House is white with the plumage of robes.
One day, two, it may be a week before the film of death
clogs in their cheeks and they are carried to the logs,
stacked like stones with millet and barley to burn.
Some take as many as five hours. Two men tend to the body
that blazes; five hundred rupees to snap before the temple.
The poor and swollen below the bridge. In Nepal
one must lie close to the river of ashes.

Still more children fly from rocks above the river, stab the water
and rise in a cackle of joy. Clothes trickle in and out of the liquid,
dry on the reeds. The pads rise from the water like gray thumbs,
and each day the murmur of death descends upon their flat faces.
For two thousand years they have waded a river too strong for Shiva,
and when it spills into the Ganges, for India. Water buffalo surge
its banks, burst forth a snarl of air, ride the minerals and mud
to a pool where they seize the last strobe of sun from Annapurna.
Cars cloak the streets and buses throttle ashes to sky.
No one comes to the river without a careful knotting.
Even the dogs listen for the scrawl of water on death's distant shore.
Women, thinned with pride, turn the few drops of wet into urns and walk
the streets that empty to homes. But always they go,
laughing with children in a wrinkle of quiet feet.

From *Winter in Pediatrics* (2006)

It Was Not Blame

Of all the voices wishing flight
from their beds, the smallest dreams
at my side, head hutched in their flying hands,
the volley of sweet nameless faces
who push her back to this world,
to crest the day without a tear,
that which slips from her eye,
child of the unfinished marriage.

It was not blame
who steered her young life over
the precipice, how we try
in grief's aftermath
to navigate the shallows of her life,
the rudderless work of mother,
slow, dreamless step-taking
to the other side
of autumn's waiting hand.

Mosquitoes

They squeak and squirt and squiggle
in my arms. Mosquitoes, they refuse
to go away. They link the room
with the suck and burp of bottles,
infants who writhe on the feather

that brought them to intensive care.
They swim in the palms of nurses
to slake the thirst of days under glass.
The names on the headboards
collect the first spots of milk.

For the whole of their short lives,
the words are gone, the vowels
slip to oxygen, the violet storm
of memory almost disguised
for the hours of lying alone.

Rooms

I

What room do you come from,
child of the broken lung?

And you, hockey player
whispered open by a stroke?

The family gathered bedside,
the chorus singing father's name.

II

Husband of sixty years,
he lay in this place not two months ago.
He gestures under fluorescent light:
hematoma, pacemaker. She believes
him, but they are not words.

They idle the chords of the long-married.
He intimates a kiss, a squeezed hand.
She rehearses the word for love.
It is the first word she will speak,
his name on her tongue since the 40s.

She regards the loss of time
to ordinary events as beadwork,
like breathing or waiting for the weight
of blankets. This, behind the draped
outline of a man with her ring.

In the Tent of Miracles

I have no words for your heart
already halved at four months.
You live in the tent of miracles,
sent from a family of teachers
and engineers who labor in fields
of fast food. Your eyes swim
between mother and uncle who waded
through two hospitals in two states
to waste the worry of dying.
Tú eres su milagro,

but you must know that—smallest of six
whose hands have yet to touch
the frost out the window,
the birch leaves cartwheeling to ground,
like you, Nestor, to wake
in a room of natural light and sound.
You are almost old enough to love
the hands that hold your girth:
her hands, she of the old soil, she
who daily folds your heart in her arms.

Driving to the Forest After Work

Before you were cut from the day,
you drove to the forest

ready to run—and running—
however still in the morphine night,

cross the cotton dressing,
disguise the erratic stitches

as if they were stars,
inch closer to family

gathered this Christmas
near the purple rings that rise

up your leg to a loft of pillows,
for what relief might come.

Without Adolescence

Your parents, the ones who want
to ask how you drank cheap rum
on the football field

in the hope of waking
without adolescence—
they were ordinary, your parents.

They held nothing in the green fields
of chalk lines. They wanted something
other than glass to tarnish the night.

They wanted the flesh of one boy
before the swimming began,
before the angel of recovery

limped into the room and blew
you back to the question
they could not ask.

The Heart Donor

I

You whisper into the forest of small hearts,
the marriage of finite halves in your chest.
You wait for a call that will save—
the flight to surgeon who will seam skin
with the organ of another. The odds of undoing
are precise: for you to live, one must die
on a fingerprint, the muscle jigsaw to lungs.

You are a woman at the breast of another,
her face a diary of unfinished labor.
A collage of names awaits her—mother, worker,
woman who speaks with her unborn children—
the chemistry of waiting for the unknown,
as yet unloved, but she will wake you,
kiss the brow of your lithe frame
and answer with her life. She will rest one from two,
close your hands as you start to thank her
and follow to old age.

II

She who receives will not know how it came.
She will not know what car you were driving,
what word you spoke before breath entered for the last time.
She will name you mother and you will unfold in her
the wisdom of your half-life, the quizzical turntable
that found you donor, lifted from lungs that she might
always breathe your first word in thanks. There will be no silence
to commemorate the algorithm of pulse to pain.
She will fold a letter and wish it to arrive at your door
but you will not be there. You will answer with your life—

and she become what each could not,
the metronome of two hearts undone.

The Unwanted Cowboy

It is the anniversary of Ghandi's death,
the sky has shorn all color but blue and
white stars below the halo of daybreak.

At the hospital, she perforates the weight
of him in her arms, the immigrant student
he stripped to no woman. She marks this day

with Ghandi's sadness, the taste
of flesh bent to dust in the new world.
I gather wood and think of her scaled to ribs—

what must she confide to the desert?
Her mouth is a moon for the loss of words
hunched over the rim of the eastern sky.

Watch Him Disappear

Nestor, each day you disappear
into the folds of medicine,
your throat tubed to oxygen,
the lemon liquid taped to your chest.
I touch your fingers and your eyes
perk open. You have found new stories
to believe in. Some wishes
you spell with your small hands.

Outside, a dove calls to no one from the spruce.
I think of the monitors that engineer
your hours clipped to bedside,
how you blur the air of intimacy
to feel mother's love. She is not
in the room, but hears you always.
The blue scripture of veins pinch her chest,
the imperfect blossom of your heart.

She empties her purse to call someone,
anyone, to the only moment—*now,*
the calendar of imperfect things.

The Iris Ballet

The light over Mt. Rose combs the irises
on the sill. Your mother grows twelve
varieties of the violet rainbow.
She has given twenty-two years
to unwind your body. Under the blankets,
your feet twist to cloth,
braid the tubes of aquarium sounds.

There are four hands to clear your airway
of the words *I can't breathe,* your face
a pillow for lying under silence.
You draw stories with their hands
and she holds your legs, says, *don't worry*
as the pulse races, says *your friend*
will come soon to trick clocks into believing

tomorrow, says your MD is genetic,
passed *from me,* as if she could take
the consonants from your lungs.

The Record of Hands

In nine months I have not touched
these hands; they are worry stones:

my neighbor drove forty miles to fetch
a Valentine flower and rolled his truck;

a co-worker's husband waived off
rehab in a downtown motel.

They mimic the inchoate stares of lying
without love. The reasons do not lie down.

My neighbor pulls oxygen to his mouth,
my co-worker shelters her daughter

from the blaze of neon in the sky. Friends,
they cannot answer the persistent absence

of who they are: hands closed to mine,
what the priest calls the stain of living.

Have they any other living? In the time
a child gestates, I have not held its shadow.

Witness to Questions

She waits in a dressing gown—beyond
the odorless white of biopsy and diagnosis.
Her son wants to know if she will change,
asks if she will have "wooden boobs."

In the support group, they welcome the survivor's
laugh, measure the consequence of a day
without suffering. The witnesses to questions
comfort what medicine cannot.

She breathes a memory into the air:
"I am alone with two children—
after the hospital, I need the day to go on."

Sister to the Vine

for Chelise

She is fallen from the vine of their lives,
mother and father who, but for the tubes
that spider her arms, name this day hers.
A near-woman now, she is the daughter
of many tissues, the girl who knots
flesh with her eyes—quivers what is
expected, like sand after water.
She recreates herself with the halo

of a gesture, finds the circle of family
in the mountains beyond the room.
For the ones who listen, she has a voice:
it is the ephemeral touch of sound to skin,
her lightening sound that will not go away.
She murmurs the fits of staying, of lying
bedside for what she will become, sister
to the vine, so many lives has she led.

Last Night We Were Told War Is Imminent

Sleepless, I left for the hospital—
the desert of others awakened to dust.
I could not repair to the dreamless and
saw a mountain bluebird: our bird of paradise.

We live where wind eats bristlecone stumps,
where no water sprouts from stone,
where snowflakes in the March night
come as memory of a time before this.

In an eastern room I sat with him—
his bike tipped to dust in the Lovelock desert.
In weeks the swelling will go down,
skin grafts appease the darkness of his leg.

By the time he returns to ride, the bluebird
will have flown its sage perch, the desert of others
scrubbed silent. How like a bluebird
is the patina of skin without shrapnel.

After Surgery

for S.

Today, a young man asked for food
at the hospital. I was without money,
having just learned of your surgery:
from you, they took the taste of food.

This, to stay alive in the bare wire
of living beyond cancer. There are
no rules in this moment without choice.
You raise a lung to receive loved ones,

and the sour breath endures the flight
from testimony to patience—
you have come to the arbor's edge
and here must tend a new field.

The daffodils will persist, the daylight
enfold what has become woman. I think
of the hundred fields tended by women
who turn the subtle over and over in their palms

to remake the morning for each other, for
the long white indifference at the door.

Programmer

for Bill

Days ago, he flew the dirt in his Landcruiser,
wrote programs for the tunnel of ideas.
Into the house of living things, he wedged
a presence: she knew what this time meant.

When the first rain came, the dust bloomed
in a field of other tasks and the waiting began.
Once this day was over, the rain settled among
the small hands of their son. *My father*

may not make it—he needed no translation.
For the next many months, they waited
at the door of questions. The furious doctoring,
the full light of weather about to descend.

I have wished for reasons to explain the person
who sleeps at the edge of failed health. The swing
from here to hour's end lies under his tongue—
the life-word I, a wafer that disappears.

Survivor

a found poem for S.

It's hard to get used to the idea

of not dying—

should I renew

this subscription,

plan for Christmas?

For six months

the killing cloud rode my flesh

to a last, prescient lie:

I might live

to abide its sorrow.

Today, I am a woman restored—

if not to health,

to the idea of tomorrow

without death.

Father to an Imaginary Grandson

With each swallow of orange juice
you migrate from the easy chair.

The caregiver wanders eight feet
for you, faint, dressed for the visit

with your child and her children.
Your grandson kicks from the stroller—

he wants to ride your chair—
his two years are extant.

What divinity regards such loss:
you have no name for him—

he suspends the chart in the hall:
today, there are no memories.

What the years engraved,
don't matter, grandpa,

as if to say, you got me
to pinch death's indifference.

Lunch with the Trabajadoras

Chica Mala sends her friends the signal—
he speaks Spanish—*¿Te quieres un poco?*
No, no se puedo—voy a mi casa.

In that moment the hospital is varicose:
the floors and railings they sweep and dust
to keep the young and not so young

from dying. A family of five
share this table when the sun permits—
the rattle of Spanglish over *dinero,*

puro dinero. They eat the lunch hour
with incantations until
Chica Mala relents and lets me in,

as if I could choose to leave
the piecework of women in the brown
and white far north of Nevada.

In the Chaplain's Shadow

She's a frequent flyer—in and out
of the hospital, her dialysis a swim
to land with the ebb and flow of fluid.

This is my friend, she begins, *a poet—*
I think of poets as prophets. In the haze
of recovery, the woman stirs a hello

from her tongue. I join their hands
in prayer and do not understand
the weight upon either woman.

Seized by the order of the cross
the chaplain is like belief—her cloth
confounds the heart without hope.

I remember the Greek Orthodox
symbol tiled at our feet in Naxos,
how it held the incantation

of belief to stone, wisdom which
becomes prayer to the patient. I watch
her hand in the palm of sorrow,

the flesh to whom she vows relief.
We are kin to loss, but we are not lost—
she confides and closes her visit.

How She Works

for Becky

On this floor, the fifth above earth,
she caroms from the desk to a girl

whose cast licks skin to steel and
in her cartoon suit the cast becomes

a wand to whisk the elevator
to waiting family. Downstairs,

at lunch with her daughter, there is
a quarter hour for the flight of swings

before the comet of young lives, torn
from the hotel of absent parents, resumes.

She stops their eyes with a grin—the ruby
light of work begins: *I'm here—*

tell me your story. She has already given
this time to an unfinished labor,

as if overcome with the dominion
of children, who slant in metal beds,

wait to hear the one right sound: *Go home.*
The fear is done. You are strong.

Song for Wilena

You bubble into rounds
with cheekfuls of praise
for the children
who hide and wink—
the Scottish nurse
who shields them
from the pegs
of medicine.

For months
you sabered with cells
in the wild of your body
until one morning,
on the subject of diet,
you announced
to all low-carb sinners,
I have chained the fridge shut.

Wilena, namesake
of the island to poets
hungered by fog—
your face is rounder this day,
as if a child
aged in your midst.
We kiss you now
and leave the leaving to family.

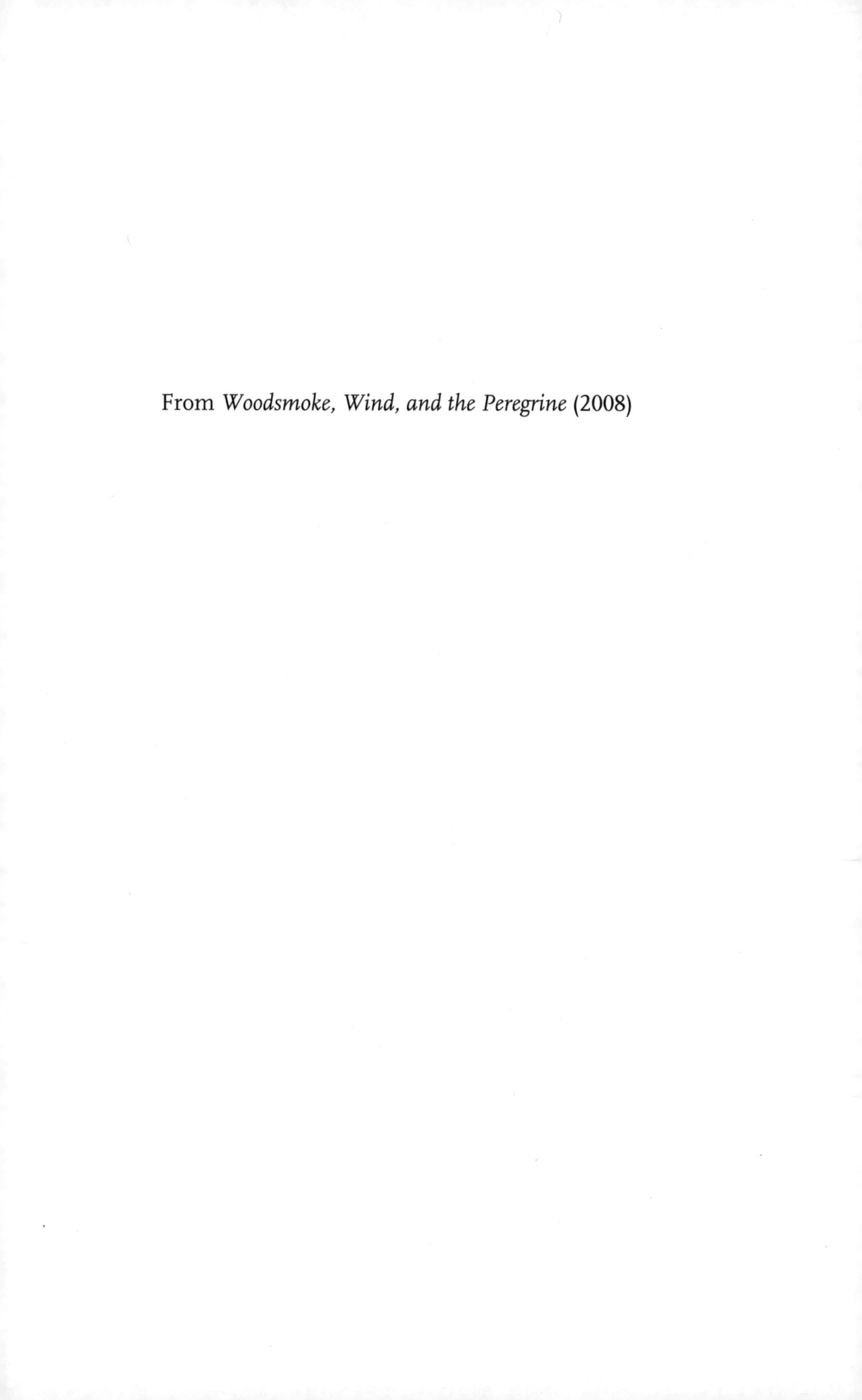

From *Woodsmoke, Wind, and the Peregrine* (2008)

First Light, Collioure

The birds motion to stars
come down, come down.

A trumpeter swan
divines the light.

A faint crescent
tears at the horizon.

Far away, Icarus climbs
from his wooden bed.

The ritual migration
from particle to animal.

And the waning dark
lifts to wings.

The Blue Heron at First Light

for J.

Twice you folded the melancholy light
with wings: once for my brother, once
for the world that will not speak to him.

The tender piers of Wilmington
beguiled the ocean dark; still you dared
to nest amidst the rotting wood.

We boys crept the planks to a tapered bill
that slowly wheezed the awkward chill.
My dear, bony kin pierced the distance

between bird and water for seconds
till your pewter tips broke for cover
to glide the Spartan masts. When he

reached for wings a second time,
you moved like a needle of the night
to lift the solitary beak to sky.

He never turned to raid the egg at rest.
The channel wedged the half of you
to crown the isle of wood: his flesh

wingless and yours, nearly weightless
save the residue of gray feathers
that strangely came to comfort him.

If there were but station or friend
he would strike like a predator to feed,
yet moments after your great carriage

rose, I saw him lose at first light
the will to fly, even as the sun
came to cradle the reeds of your skin.

The Last Songbird on Malta

for Doc, for the Malta songbirds
hunted for sport

All night, the glorious footsteps of rain
on Spanish tiles, the persistent reminder
of moisture from sky. In the arid hill
country of France, the night damp
came as cold messenger.
Then daylight. We opened
the shutters to a sparrow
in the eucalyptus.

I heard
the last songbird on Malta, broken
from the melodious chant of wings.
And how we must survive
"the immaculate voice of extinction."
I am wont to recreate its sound,
the empty grief before light.

Even carrier pigeons, sworn in their flock,
mark the vines with hope.
But for the three sparrows
in the wisteria at St. Julian's, the chatter
soars from memory. Not theirs, but kin
splintered by errant island shells.
And now the bird mending, the tireless
restraint to stay alive.

Who must sing
for the last of their tribe?
The echo of starvation
regards a wing as friend of hunger.
On the island of stone and flowers,
the songbird heeds the infinite cry:
leave me this wing of peace.

Resurrection

The last to leave
after magpie, vulture—

the crow rises from asphalt
to the carnival existence.
He presumes innocence
in the warm cathedral,
the catechism of the dark.

The ash of wings
stretch sky.
He masks the mercy
of strangers and sees no light
beyond his own.

If you survive
he will dispense with ceremony,
caw a single plaintive note,
and release you
to the highway of lingering hands.

Hummingbird

At twelve I raised the barrel not six feet from eyes,
the first gun I fired, a .22 caliber,
and still in flight you twisted to earth
filled with a shell the size of your bill.

That day, years ago, I thought you dead
for all time. Now you dive the back yard peach,
wibbling and wobbling over nectar, your
greenish-blue coat lost in a fluorescent whir.

Sixty times a second you delight, and no hunter,
save the memory of boys flying the sight
of an old gun. I smell your burnt flesh
on the bough, and the butt kicks my shoulder

like the one that cut you down.
For a time, I wished you never return
and the wash behind my parent's house
fold in sage. But in the clearing where you flutter

you teach me to forgive a long-ago boy
when he, on a dare, pulled you from sky
and snaked blood from lime feathers.
You teach me to forgive the scar

we leave on land with wings.

Ode to Carmen's Chickens

from Peru to Tuesday
on the Comstock

The cock crows from Carmen's hutch,
I crow with it, happy to be back.
I stood the many fences shaking
and found no altar to redeem,
took the bushy red muezzin
and let the feathers free—
the fragile door of daylight
we must step through
to live in the desert.

There are no caracoles here.
A narwhal tusk will never poke
from the mine shafts.
Coil springs and bed frames lie penitent
before the toil of home.
The inland sea has dried, the Paiute
hunters long dead in their caves.
I mark my cave with silence
rejoice in the absence of trickery

before the world closes
once again. And march
the veiled shawl of winter
to behold the Peruvian dust on my skin
still flaking from switchbacks
to the labyrinth of Andean stone.
I walked long to find my home.
It is here, on the porch, in deep August sun
soiled with chickens and leaves.

Red-Tail in a Snow Field

The burnished wing,
the rusted tail
arc the sky
to wood
and earth.

How many more
cut the horizon
with flight?
Imagine
each red star
fallen to ash.

Ezra's Crow

I

At twenty I walked the orange grove
from college reading Ezra Pound
till black from treetop came
the shrill weight of sound.
But there was no malice
to forgive, only the scented
air of hardwood and crow,
naked before the city. Audacious bird—
what snares a wing to grief?

II

Driving the tender desert home
the crows have followed
from Phelan to Pear Blossom
through a winter draw: shadow birds
anoint the wellspring of sorrow.

III

There is no flight left
to soothe its brow—
the ash of wings rise
to scuttle the abiding light
of late November. If crow
could tell, it would be in pictographs
like Pound, the hazel sky bent
to marrow, with scant food to follow.

IV

Fickle in flight,
hearsay on the wind,
if it could tell the bolt
of feathers, my eyes
would recoil at such red:
beak that scowls to gullet
is surely huff to weaker kin.
If not, what other death
such a heinous cry portends?

V

All the way home cheated by absence,
Ezra gone like the orange wood,
the crow not yet flown.
A silence sings to bone.
No tally of wings
will presume innocence
for crow, for poet.
At this altitude the feral quill has fallen.

The Goldfinches at Mid-Morning

Here in the firelight of pine sun,
of black oak sun, more yellow
than canary breasts, came four—

timid first, then beating the black
dam of thistle and what all my mother-
in-law found at the drug store—

I read the lawless news of Andrea,
a single mother who danced
the winded caves of Sacramento

bars to feed a child. And twisted
with the she-mother preening:
would I finger a twenty

for her fiery dream of law school?
Tufted in lace, her lines a ritual
for the sleeper train to Syracuse,

for the daughter she must leave
to fight the nest of failure.
And will the goldfinches find her

knocking bargains from the dime store
when she is but a stranger
in the tangled light of a city?

When the Buttons Leave for School

When buttons swing for the door,
when boys but corner the pole
and pinch the clouds to school,

when free on feet, they swagger
the ditches, ducking and twitching
like a covey of quail,

when the mighty shadow of legs
boils to steps,
they hook the hole in the road

dreaming the playground
has fallen to popsicles
that cross the lips with icy red.

And when the talons
pounce the last to leave,
oh smallest bird, my child,

you will skip to sage
and fire a magical lance
goodbye. And huddle

with numbers and letters
and wasted events that crook
the wings to the cornice of age.

The Snowy Egret Slough

Father, you followed me to Chile.
Today, in the slough, the snowy egret
still as rice, waiting for shadow,

for insect to glaze the surface of water,
the crustacean fingers below gray sky,
and my family plods behind me,

a ruddy duck at best, no grace
in my standing as you pierce
the inlet with each pointed print,

a lingering memory of us
muddled in the shallows, my kin
too little to understand

we forget our fathers to free them,
until the river surges, narrowly
gorged from rock in Isla Negra,

the plover birds etch the silt,
and I wade the smoky bottom
but cannot follow: your white

powder wings lift to sky—
my shadow family falls to mist, and I
start the river home without you.

Releasing Sparrows at the Buddhist Temple

for Stephen Shu-Ning Liu

For 20 baht, the bird woman opens the cage,
releases six sparrows to the saffron light
and chants, *Good luck will follow all your days.*

I thought of you in Hainan, paying cents
to free a snowy egret from the farmer's hatchet,
the farmer who shook in disbelief, *Stupid man*—

but how could he know your grandfather
was a yellow crane released to the long ago
fiction of home, and you, caged in the gilded temple

of the desert, loose all wings in your path
to wake with family and teach a literature
so few will read. And hasn't it always been hard

for birds, and some would say, for us?
You fool the temple dwellers, cross the Yangtze
to freedom, then light on foreign land,

the yellow crane no one understands.
And the flight begins: beneath the scurvy
of survival, each day a piece of luck.

Emerald Lake

Campfire, cook stove, cold mountain.
Not far from Han Shan, my boys and I
on a glacial cirque, the youngest
twitching the Ugly Stik, the sacred
golden trout inches below the surface.

On what green splinters do we lay our lives?
Pine bough, alpine lake, stumpy moon.
Overhead, a falcon sweeps sky, and
last night the haunting wings
in our camp—was he wounded or hiding?

I reason with the marks of work and men
most of the year, but today, smoke-filled
and arguably the happiest I've been, relinquish
my stern hold on things and clutter the lake
with my bones, the three of us, cold naked stones.

Postcard to Wally Easterly From Here in the Loneliest Town on Highway 50

Nevada unfolds
to snow cloud
barnacle ridge
still water
inked with dry mountains.

All day the burrowing
sky eats the last
hours of April.

Mile-markers cut the road edge:
white flags
with no country to bear
save greasewood and alkaline flats.

We swim the desert's black skin
a highway of turtles
turned belly up,
the milky stomachs
vulnerable to flesh-eating birds.

What I would give
for a raven on my chest.

Waking from the Charcoal Dark

    for A.

The birdhouse beckons
                    but no bird will nest
        "at blackberrying time"
the pine cone swings from twine
        girded with peanut butter and sesame seed
                    for winds yet to blow
the old wooded sky crowds to comfort
                    these few hours Sunday morning
        before the crack of an ax
all breath hinged on a tree limb
        and my son flies a string of leaves
to the ground.

A phone call from the prison cell
        empties the room: the web begins
        to unravel. They too were boys.

Last night in the broken dark
                    the flashing of a friend
stretchered from helicopter to hospital
and this morning every line I read
        from a fine Vermont poet
seems the horned owl blinking
                    at the devious clotting
        of charlatans holding forth
and I cannot pretend—let them pronounce
the death of dreams. I must get on with my life.

The sun rides the juniper
                    harnessed with silver berries
the locust spines
        pierce flesh to remind:

morning has come. Let them fiddle
the four corners of doom. I must thread
the road with blackberries, worm the apples
and close my fingers in soil, this before breakfast
          on Sunday morning.

The Loons on Walker Lake

Already, you know this story will end
in the glands of waterfowl
digging the metallic river.

Now one hundred years gone,
the stamp mill's dirge
is a flute beneath the silt.

The unlucky loon
volunteers nothing from shore,
and I remember Twain

who likened us to loons
in the saline brine
before the mines went down,

this river become lake
to loons with no surface
for the patina of gold.

The Grey Elliot Riff

Not the whiskered breath of Umatilla
	scudding the range
or the foggy river out your door
but the way you swam Hopkins
	and cummings, upstream
"mud-luscious" to the floor.

Not the wrinkled print of stilt
	in the Stan Field slough
or the cowbirds tented on the post
but the soft flush of Monica
	sailing from Cimmiyotti's,
that late ride to the bar.

Not the pounding of pileated
	pecker on the musty volumes
or writers wintered in the shed
but the way you closed the spring
	to college after so long
a learned life in its maw.

Not the dragon magpies piercing
	the feckless wheat
or the inky halo from a plow
but a drift on the John Day
	with ample repose—
king of the sanded bar

lilting in a poem by the shore.

City of Gray

at the church of the catacombs, Lima

The city of gray slows to sun,
the apricot buildings peel to stone.
Pigeons swarm the square like children

and tossing kernels to feed them
I think of the Quechua proverb:
Ama suwa, ama llulla, ama q'ella—

don't steal, don't lie, don't laze.
If such wisdom could exist
my mouth would tarnish

with the telling, but the child
and the pigeon do not hide:
the fog has curled to let them fly.

Tanager

For seven years you have lived in my wood,
and twice seven before that idle moment
the first yellow wing sloped to pine,
incredulous then at such radiant flight,
I fled the hope of seeing you again.

Were it mine to choose, I would name
you fireweed, or tanager, or woman,
but it is not mine. You have many
names and like the bird so long ago flown,
they have aged into colors not yet known—

colors you would feather
if it were flight and not my hand
embraced so young. Now I ring
the forest with memory and see her only
thrice these waning years:

the spectral bird having flushed
the two of us from our dens
to mate and moan and marry
the distal silence when each could send
a wing to sweep the widening door.

Not as messenger did she come,
but woman to spring the waiting flesh.
How is it a pastel bird can wince
the years to rest, and so doing,
wake the waiting flesh? She can.

On the Porch

The sparrows are racketing
          high in the feeder
and I am low in the saddle
          of a book, not one
but many wings tethered to seed.

Late Harvest Without Moon

Nothing is over
all limbs bob, the piñon jay
corks three fat apples.

The Ornithologist's Prayer

Neruda would not have named you,

Vallejo gone mad before weeping a lie,

and I

will not give breath to the rhetorical end

in sight:

no bird shall repair

to the coded history

of wings,

etch the skeletal

mosaic of time

with its silence.

Colophon

Designed and produced by Robert Blesse at the Black Rock Press, Department of Art, School of the Arts, University of Nevada, Reno.

The text typeface is Scala, an old style, humanist, serif typeface designed by Dutch typeface designer Martin Majoor in 1990 for the Vredenburg Music Center in Utrecht, the Netherlands. It is named for the Teatro alla Scala in Milan, Italy. The display typeface on the cover and title page is Mrs. Eaves, a transitional serif typeface designed by Zuzana Licko in 1996. It is a revival of the types of English printer and punchcutter John Baskerville, and is named for his longtime housekeeper and collaborator, Sarah Eaves, whom eventially became his wife.

Printed by Thomson Shore, Dexter, Michigan